FUNDAMENTALS
OF PROSPERITY

FUNDAMENTALS OF PROSPERITY

ROGER W. BABSON

WILDSIDE PRESS

FUNDAMENTALS OF PROSPERITY

Copyright © 1920.

Published in 2007 by Wildside Press.
www.wildsidepress.com

FOREWORD

Some two thousand years ago the greatest teacher who ever walked the earth advised the people of Judea not to build their houses on the sand. What he had in mind was that they were looking too much to the structure above ground, and too little to the spiritual forces which must be the foundation of any structure which is to stand. Following the war we enjoyed the greatest prosperity this country has ever witnessed — the greatest activity, the greatest bank clearings, the greatest foreign trade, the greatest railroad gross earnings, the highest commodity prices.

We then constructed a ten-story building on a foundation meant for only a two or three story building. Hence the problem confronting us business men is to strengthen the foundation or else see the structure fall. I am especially glad of the opportunity to write for business men. There are two reasons: first, because I feel that the business men are largely responsible for having this ten-story structure on a foundation made for one of only two or three stories; secondly, because I believe such men alone have the vision, the imagination and the ability to strengthen the foundation and prevent the structure from falling.

The fact is, we have become crazy over material things. We are looking only at the structure above ground. We are trying to get more smoke from the chimney. We are looking at space instead of service, at profits instead of volume. With our eyes focused on the structure above ground, we have lost sight of those human resources, thrift, imagination, integrity, vision and faith which make the structure possible. I feel that only by the business men can this foundation be strengthened before the inevitable fall comes.

When steel rails were selling at $55 a ton, compared with only $25 a ton a few years previous, our steel plants increased their capacity twenty-five percent. Increased demand, you say? No, the figures don't show it. Only thirty-one million tons were produced in 1919, compared with thirty-nine million tons in 1916. People have forgotten the gospel of service. The producing power per man has fallen off from fifteen to twenty per cent. We have all been keen on developing consumption. We have devoted nine-tenths of our thought, energy and effort to developing consumption. This message is to beg of every reader to give more thought to developing production, to the reviving of a desire to produce and the realization of joy in production.

We are spending millions and millions in every city to develop the good-will of customers, to develop in customers a desire to buy. This is all well and good, but we can't continue to go in one direction indefinitely. We cannot always get steam out of the boiler without feeding the furnace. The time has come when in our own interests, in the interests of our communities, our industry, and of the nation itself, for a while we must stop adding more stories to this structure. Instead, we must strengthen the foundations upon which the entire structure rests.

R. W. B.

I

Honesty or Steel Doors?

While fifty-one per cent of the people have their eyes on the goal of integrity, our investments are secure; but with fifty-one per cent of them headed in the wrong direction, our investments are valueless. The first fundamental of prosperity is Integrity.

*

While on a recent visit to Chicago, I was taken by the president of one of the largest banks to see his new safety deposit vaults. He described these — as bank presidents will — as the largest and most marvellous vaults in the city. He expatiated on the heavy steel doors and the various electrical and mechanical contrivances which protect the stocks and bonds deposited in the institution.

While at the bank a person came in to rent a box. He made the arrangements for the box, and a box was handed to him. In it he deposited some stocks and bonds which he took from his pocket. Then the clerk who had charge of the vaults went to a rack on the wall and took out a key and gave it to the man who had rented the box. The man then put the box into one of the little steel compartments, shut the door and turned the key. He then went away feeling perfectly secure on account of those steel doors and various mechanical and electrical contrivances existing to protect his wealth.

I did not wish to give him a sleepless night so I said nothing; but I couldn't help thinking how easy it would have been for that poorly-paid, humpbacked clerk to make a duplicate of that key before he delivered it to the renter of that box. With such a duplicate, the clerk could have made that man penniless within a few minutes after he had left the building. The great steel door and the electrical and mechanical contrivances would have been absolutely valueless.

Of course the point I am making is that the real security which that great bank in Chicago had to offer its clientele lay not in the massive stone columns in front of its structure; nor in the heavy steel doors; nor the electrical and mechanical contrivances. The real strength of that institution rested in the honesty — the absolute integrity — of its clerks.

******

That afternoon I was talking about the matter with a business man. We were discussing securities, earnings and capitalization. He seemed greatly troubled by the mass of figures before him. I said to him: "Instead of pawing over these earnings and striving to select yourself the safest bond, you will do better to go to a reliable banker or bond-house and leave the decision with him."

"Why," he said, "I couldn't do that."

"Mr. Jones," I went on, "tell me the truth! After you buy a bond or a stock certificate, do you ever take the trouble to see if it is signed and countersigned properly? Moreover, if you find it signed, is there any way by which you may know whether the signature is genuine or forged?"

"No," he said, "there isn't. I am absolutely dependent on the integrity of the bankers from whom I buy the securities."

And when you think of it, there is really no value at all in the pieces of paper which one so carefully locks up in these safety deposit boxes. There is no value at all in the bank-book which we so carefully cherish. There is no value at all in those deeds and mortgages upon which we depend so completely. The value rests *first*, in the integrity of the lawyers, clerks and stenographers who draw up the papers; *secondly*, in the integrity of the officers who sign the documents; *thirdly*, in the integrity of the courts and judges which would enable us to enforce our claims; and *finally*, in the integrity of the community which would determine whether or not the orders of the court will be executed.

These things which we look upon as of great value: the stocks, bonds, bank-books, deeds, mortgages, insurance policies, etc., are merely nothing. While fifty-one per cent. of the people have their eyes on the goal of Integrity, our investments are secure; but with fifty-one per cent. of them headed in the wrong direction, our investments are valueless. So the first fundamental of prosperity is integrity. Without it there is no civilization, there is no peace, there is no security, there is no safety. Mind you also that this applies just as much to the man who is working for wages as to the capitalist and every owner of property.

Integrity, however, is very much broader than the above illustration would indicate. Integrity applies to many more things than to money. Integrity requires the seeking after, as well as the dispensing of, truth. It was this desire for truth which founded our educational institutions, our sciences and our arts. All the great professions, from medicine to engineering, rest upon this spirit of integrity. Only as they so rest, can they prosper or even survive.

Integrity is the mother of knowledge. The desire for truth is the basis of all learning, the value of all experience and the reason for all study and investigation. Without integrity as a basis, our entire educational system would fall to the ground; all newspapers and magazines would become sources of great danger and the publication of books would have to be suppressed. Our whole civilization rests upon the assumption that people are honest. With this confidence shaken, the structure falls. And it should fall, for, unless the truth be taught, the nation would be much better off without its schools, newspapers, books and professions. Better have no gun at all, than one aimed at yourself. The corner-stone of prosperity is the stone of Integrity.

II

Faith the Searchlight of Business

This religion which we talk about for an hour a
week, on Sunday, is not only the vital force which
protects our community, but it is the vital force
which makes our communities. The power of our
spiritual forces has not yet been tapped.

*

About three years ago I was travelling in South
America. When going from Sao Paulo up across the
tablelands to Rio Janeiro, I passed through a little
poverty-stricken Indian village. It was some 3,000 feet
above sea level; but it was located at the foot of a great
water-power. This water-power, I was told, could
easily develop from 10,000 to 15,000 horse-power for
twelve months of the year. At the base of this waterfall
lived these poverty-stricken Indians, plowing their
ground with broken sticks, bringing their corn two
hundred miles on their backs from the seacoast, and
grinding it by hand between two stones. Yet — with a
little faith and vision, they could have developed that
water-power, even though in a most primitive man-
ner, and with irrigation, could have made that poverty-stricken valley a veritable Garden of Eden. They
simply lacked *faith*. They lacked vision. They were
unwilling, or unable, to look ahead to do something
for the next generation and trust to the Lord for the
results.

I met the head man of the village and said to him:
"Why is it that you don't do something to develop this
power?"

"Why, if we started to develop this thing," he an-
swered, "by the time we got it done, we would be
dead."

Indians had lived there for the last two hundred years lacking the vision. No one in that community had the foresight or vision to think or see beyond the end of his day. It was lack of faith which stood between them and prosperity. Hence, the second great fundamental of prosperity is that intangible "something," — known as faith, vision, hope, whatever you may call it.

The writer of the Book of Proverbs says: "Where there is no vision, the people perish." Statistics teach that where there is no vision, civilization never gets started! The tangible things which we prize so highly — buildings, railroads, steamships, factories, power plants, telephones, airplanes, etc., are but the result of faith and vision. These things are only symptoms of conditions, mere barometers which register the faith and vision of mankind.

This religion which we talk about for an hour a week, on Sunday, is not only the vital force which protects our community, but it is the vital force which *makes* our communities. *The power of our spiritual forces has not yet been tapped!* Our grandchildren will look back upon us and wonder why we neglected our trust and our opportunity, just as we look back on those poor Indians in Brazil who plowed with crooked sticks, grinding their corn between stones and hauling it on their backs two hundred miles from the seaboard.

******

These statements are not the result of any special interest as a churchman. I am not a preacher. I am simply a business man, and my work is almost wholly for bankers, brokers, manufacturers, merchants and investors. The concern with which I am associated has one hundred and eighty people in a suburb of Boston who are collecting, compiling and distributing statistics on business conditions. We have only one source of income, and that is from the clients who pay us for an analysis of the situation. Therefore you may rest assured that it is impossible for us to do any propaganda work in the interests of any one nation, sect, religion or church. The only thing we can give clients is a conclusion based on a diagnosis of a given situation. As probably few of you readers are clients of ours, may I quote from a Bulletin which we recently sent to these bankers and manufacturers?

"The need of the hour is not more legislation. The need of the hour is more religion. More religion is needed everywhere, from the halls of Congress at Washington, to the factories, the mines, the fields and the forests. It is one thing to talk about plans or policies, but a plan or policy without a religious motive is like a watch without a spring or a body without the breath of life. The trouble, today, is that we are trying to hatch chickens from sterile eggs. We may have the finest incubator in the world and operate it according to the most improved regulations — moreover, the eggs may appear perfect specimens — but unless they have the germ of life in them all our efforts are of no avail."

I have referred to the fact that the security of our investments is absolutely dependent upon the faith, the righteousness and the religion of other people. I have stated that the real strength of our investments is due, not to the distinguished bankers of America, but rather to the poor preachers. I now go farther than that and say that the development of the country as a whole is due to this *something*, this indescribable *something*, this combination of faith, thrift, industry, initiative, integrity and vision, which these preachers have developed in their communities.

Faith and vision do not come from the wealth of a nation. It's the faith and vision which produce the wealth. The wealth of a country does not depend on its raw materials. Raw materials are to a certain extent essential and to a great extent valuable; but the nations which today are richest in raw materials are the poorest in wealth. Even when considering one country — the United States — the principle holds true. The coal and iron and copper have been here in this country for thousands of years, but only within the last fifty years have they been used. Water-powers exist even today absolutely unharnessed. Look the whole world over and there has been no increase in raw materials. There existed one thousand years ago more raw materials than we have today, but we then lacked men with a vision and the faith to take that coal out of the ground, to harness the water-powers, to build the railroads and to do other things worth while. So I say, the second great fundamental of prosperity is Faith.

III

Industry vs. Opportunity

Industry is the mother of invention. Struggle, sacrifice and burning midnight oil have produced the cotton gin, the sewing machine, the printing press, the steam engine, the electric motor, the telephone, the incandescent lamp and the other great inventions of civilization. Some religious enthusiasts think only of the "lilies of the fields" and forget the parable of the talents.

*

A few years ago I was employed by one of the largest publishing houses in the country to make a study of America's captains of industry. The real purpose of the study was to discover some industry or some man that could be helped greatly through national advertising. In connection with that study of those captains of industry, I tabulated their ancestry. These were the seventy greatest manufacturers, merchants and railroad builders, the leading men who have made America by developing the fields, the forests, the mines and the industries. What did I find? I found that only five per cent. of these captains of industry are the sons of bankers; only ten per cent. of them are the sons of manufacturers; fifteen per cent. of them are the sons of merchants, while over thirty per cent. of them are the sons of poor preachers and farmers.

Why is it that ministers' sons hold a much more important place in the industrial development of America than the sons of bankers? The ministers' sons inherit no wealth, they have no more than their share of college education; they are not especially religious as the world measures religion. In fact, there is an old saying about "ministers' sons and deacons' daughters." I would be false to my reputation as a statistician to hold up these captains of industry as saintly examples for young men to follow. But the fact remains nevertheless that these men are creating America today. Now, what's the reason?

The reason is that these men have a combination of the two traits already mentioned and a third added thereto; — namely, the habit of work. They have inherited a certain rugged integrity from their mothers and a gift of vision from their fathers which, when combined with the habit of work — forced upon them by their family's meager income — means *power*. Integrity is a dry seed until put in the ground of faith and allowed to grow. But faith with works is prosperity.

A man may be honest and wonder why he does not get ahead; a man may have vision and still remain only a dreamer; but when integrity and vision are combined with hard work, the man prospers. It is the same with classes and nations.

It has been said that genius is the author of invention. Statistics do not support this statement. The facts show that industry is the mother of invention. Struggle, sacrifice and burning midnight oil have produced the cotton gin, the sewing machine, the printing press, the steam engine, the electric motor, the telephone, the incandescent lamp and the other great inventions of civilization.

Why is it that most of the able men in our great industries came from the country districts? The reason is that the country boy is trained to work. Statistics indicate that very seldom does a child, brought up in a city apartment house, amount to much; while the children of well-to-do city people are seriously handicapped. The great educator of the previous generation was not the public school, but rather the *wood box*. Those of us parents who have not a wood box for our children to keep filled, or chores for them to do, are unfortunate.

Run through the list of the greatest captains of industry, as they come to your mind. How many of the men who are really directing the country's business gained their position through inherited wealth? You will find them astonishingly few. There is no "divine right of kings" in business. In fact, statistics show us that the very things which most people think of as advantages, namely, wealth and "not having to work" are really obstacles which are rarely surmounted.

Industry and thrift are closely allied. Economic studies show clearly that ninety-five per cent. of the employers are employers because they systematically saved money. Any man who systematically saves money from early youth automatically becomes an employer. He may employ thousands or he may have only two or three clerks in a country store, but he nevertheless is an employer. These same studies show that ninety-five per cent. of the wage workers are wage workers because they have systematically spent their money as fast as they have earned it. They of necessity remain wage workers. These are facts which no labour leader can disprove and which are exceedingly significant. This is especially striking when one considers that the employer often started out at the same wages and in the same community as his wage workers. The employer was naturally industrious and thrifty; while those who remained wage workers were not.

The development of this nation through the construction of the transcontinental railways, the financng of the western farms, and the building of our cities is largely due to the old New England doctrine that laziness and extravagance are sins. In some western communities it is popular to laugh at these New England traits; but had it not been for them, these western communities would never have existed. The industry and thrift developed by the old New England religion were the basis of our national growth.

I especially desire to emphasize this point because of the position of certain religious enthusiasts who think only of "the lilies of the field" and forget the parable of the talents. It is a fact that the third fundamental of prosperity is Industry.

IV

Cooperation — Success
by Helping the Other Fellow

Our industrial system has resulted in making
many men economic eunuchs. The salvation of
our cities, the salvation of our industries and the
salvation of our nation depend on discovering
something which will revive in man that desire to
produce and joy in production which he had instinctively when he was a small boy.

*

A few days ago I was present at a dinner of business men in Boston who were called together in order
to secure some preferential freight rates for Massachusetts. The principal theme of that gathering was to
boom Massachusetts at the expense of the rest of the
country. At the close of the dinner I was asked to give
my opinion and said: "Let us see how many things
there are in this room that we could have were we
dependent solely on Massachusetts. The chairs and
furniture are from Michigan; the cotton is from Geor-
gia; the linen from Ireland; the silver from Mexico;
the glassware from Pennsylvania; the paper from
Maine; the paint from Missouri; the clock from Con-
necticut — and so on." Finally I got the courage to ask
if there was a single thing in the room that did not
originate from some state other than Massachusetts.
Those men were absolutely helpless in finding a single
thing.

The same fact applies in a general way to every
state and every home. Look about, where you are sitting now. How many things are there in the room just
where you are — there is a table, a chair, a shoe, a coat,
a necktie, a cigar, a lampshade, a piano, a basket — for

all of these you are dependent upon others.

The same fact is true when we analyze one staple like shoes which, primarily, are made of leather. Where does the leather come from? Just follow that leather from the back of the steer until you buy it in the form of shoes. Think where that steer was raised, and where the leather was tanned. Think of all the men engaged in the industry from the cow-punchers to the salesmen in the stores. But there is more than leather involved in shoes. There is cotton in the shoe lacing and lining. There is metal in the nails and eyelets. Not only must different localities cooperate to produce a shoe; but various industries must give and take likewise.

Civilization is ultimately dependent on the ability of men to cooperate. The best barometer of civilization is the desire and ability of men to cooperate. The willingness to share with others — the desire to work with others is the great contribution which Christianity has given to the world. The effect of this new spirit is most thrilling when one considers the clothes which he has on his back, the food which he has on the table, the things which he has in the house, and thinks of the thousands of people whose labour has directly contributed toward these things. Now this clearly shows that the fourth great fundamental of prosperity is cooperation, the willingness and ability of men to cooperate, to serve one another, to help one another, to give and to take.

But the teachings of Jesus along these lines have a very much broader application than when applied merely to raw materials, or even manufactured products. As we can begin to prosper only when we develop into finished products the raw materials of the fields, mines and forests, so we can become truly prosperous only as we develop the greatest of all resources — the human resources. Not only does Christianity demand that we seek to help and build up others; but our own prosperity depends thereon as well.

******

When in Washington, during the war, I had a wonderful opportunity of meeting the representatives of both labour and capital. I had some preconceived ideas on the labour question when I went to Washington; but now they are all gone. I am perfectly willing, now, to agree with the wage worker, to agree with the employer, to agree with both or to agree with neither. But this one thing I am sure of, and that is that the present system doesn't work. The present system is failing in getting men to produce.

By nature man likes to produce. Our boy, as soon as he can toddle out-of-doors, starts instinctively to make a mud pie. When he gets a little older he gets some boards, shingles and nails and builds a hut. Just as soon as he gets a knife, do you have to show him how to use it? He instinctively begins to make a boat or an arrow or perhaps something he has never seen. Why? Because in his soul is a natural desire to produce and an inborn joy in production. But what happens to most of these boys after they grow up?

Our industrial system has resulted in almost stultifying men economically and making most of them economically non-productive. Why? I don't know. I simply say it happens and the salvation of our industries depends on discovering something which will revive in man that desire to produce and that joy in production which he had instinctively when he was a small boy.

Increased wages will not do it. Shorter hours will not do it. The wage worker must feel right and the employer must feel right. It is all a question of feeling. Feelings rule this world — not things. The reason that some people are not successful with collective bargaining and profit sharing and all these other plans is because they think that men act according to what they say, or according to what they learn, or according to that in which they agree. Men act according to their *feelings*, and "good feeling" is synonymous with the spirit of cooperation. One cannot exist without the other and prosperity cannot continue without both. Hence the fourth fundamental of prosperity is *Cooperation*.

V

Our Real Resources

We have gone daffy over things like steam, electricity, water power, buildings, railroads, and ships and we have forgotten the human soul upon which all of these things depend and from which all of these things originate.

*

Two captains of industry were standing, one day, on the bridge at Niagara looking at the great falls. One man turned to the other and said: "Behold the greatest source of undeveloped power in America."

"No. The greatest source of undeveloped power in America is the soul of man," the other replied.

I was talking with a large manufacturer the other day, and he told me that he was supporting scholarships in four universities to enable young men to study the raw materials which he is using in his plant. I asked him if he was supporting any scholarships to study the human element in his plant, and he said "No." Yet when asked for definite figures, it appeared that eighty per cent. of every dollar which he spends, goes for labour, and only twenty per cent. goes for materials. He is endowing four scholarships to study the twenty per cent. and is not doing a thing to study the eighty per cent.! Statistics show that the greatest undeveloped resources in America are not our mines or our forests or our streams, but rather the human souls of the men and women who work for us.

This is most significant when one resorts to statistics and learns that everything that we have — every improvement, every railroad, every ship, every building costing in excess of $5,000, every manufacturing concern employing over twenty men, yes, every newspaper and book worth while, has originated and been developed in the minds of less than two per cent. of the people. The solution of our industrial problems and the reduction of the cost of living depend not on fighting over what is already produced, but upon producing more. This means that this two per cent. must be increased to four per cent., and then to six per cent. If all the good things which we now have, come from the enterprise of only two per cent., it is evident that we would all have three times as much if the two per cent were increased to six per cent.

Jesus was absolutely right in His contention that if we would seek first the Kingdom of God and His righteousness all these other things would naturally come to us. This is what Jesus had in mind when He urged people to give and serve, promising that such giving and serving should be returned to them a hundred fold or more. Jesus never preached unselfishness or talked sacrifice as such, but only urged His hearers to look through to the end, see what the final result would be and do what would be best for them in the long run. Jesus urged His followers to consider the spiritual things rather than the material, and the eternal things rather than the temporal; but not in the spirit of sacrifice. The only sacrifice which Jesus asked of His people was the same sacrifice which the farmer makes when he throws his seed into the soil.

The story of the loaves and fishes is still taught as a miracle, but the day will come when it will not be considered such. The same is true regarding the incident when Jesus found that His disciples had been fishing all night without results and He suggested that they cast the net on the other side. They followed His advice and the net immediately filled with so many fishes that they could hardly pull it up. If we today would give more thought to the spiritual and less to the material, we would have more in health, happiness, and prosperity. The business men today would be far better off if — like the fishermen of Galilee — we would take Jesus' advice and cast our net on "the other side."

We are told that with sufficient faith we could remove mountains. Have mountains ever been removed or tunnelled without faith? The bridging of rivers, the building of railroads, the launching of steamships, and the creation of all industries are dependent on the faith of somebody. Too much credit is given both to capital and labour in the current discussions of today. The real credit for most of the things which we have is due to some human soul which supplied the faith that was the mainspring of every enterprise. Furthermore in most instances this human soul owes this germ of faith to some little country church with a white steeple and old-fashioned furnishings.

The reason I say "old-fashioned" church is because our fathers were more willing to rely upon the power of faith than many of us today. What they lacked in many other ways was more than compensated by their faith in God. They got, through faith, "that something" which men today are trying to get through every other means. All the educators, all the psychologists, all the inspirational writers cannot put into a man the vision and the will to do things which are gained by a clear faith. Most of us today are frantically trying to invent a machine which will solve our problems, when all the while we have the machine within us, if we will only set it going. That machine is the human soul.

The great problem today is to develop the human soul, to develop this wonderful machine which each one of us has between his ears. Only as this is developed can we solve our other problems. When we give as much thought to the solution of the human problem as we give to the solution of the steam problem or the electrical problem, we will have no labour problem. We have gone daffy over things like steam, electricity, water-power, buildings, railroads and ships, and we have forgotten the human soul upon which all of these things depend and from which all of these things originate.

VI

Study the Human Soul

The first step is to give more thought and attention to people, to establish more points of contact. Let us do humanly, individually, man to man, what we are trying to do in a great big way.

*

I was visiting the home of a famous manufacturer recently and he took me out to his farm. He showed me his cattle. Above the head of each heifer and each cow was the pedigree. The most careful record was kept of every animal. He had a blue-print in his library at home of every one of those animals. Yet when we began later to talk about the labour problem in his own plant and I asked him how many of his people he knew personally, he told me — I quote his words:

"Why, they are all alike to me, Mr. Babson. I don't know one from the other."

Later in the evening — it was during the Christmas vacation — a young fellow drove up to the house in a fancy automobile, came in and asked for this manufacturer's only daughter in order to take her to a party. I didn't like the looks of the fellow very well. After they had gone out, I said to the father:

"Who is that chap?"

The father replied: "I don't know; some friend of Mary's."

The father had every one of his cows blue-printed, but he didn't know the name of the man who came to get his daughter and who didn't deliver her until two o'clock the next morning! That man was neglecting the human soul, both in his factory and in his home.

******

I repeat that we have gone crazy over structures

above ground. We are absolutely forgetting the greatest of our resources — the great spiritual resource, upon which everything depends. How shall we develop these resources?

Certainly we are not developing this great spiritual resource in the public schools. The educational system was originally founded by the Church to train the children in the fundamentals of righteousness. Gradually, but constantly, we have drifted away from this goal and today the purpose for which our schools were started has been almost entirely lost. In some states it is now a criminal offence for a school superintendent to ask a prospective school teacher what she believes or whether she has any religion whatever! Under these conditions, is it surprising that the spiritual resources of our children are lying dormant?

Much of the prosperity of this nation is due to the family prayers which were once daily held in the homes of our fathers. To a very large extent this custom has gone by. Whatever the arguments pro and con may be, the fact nevertheless remains that such family prayers nurtured and developed these spiritual resources to which the prosperity of the nation is due. The custom of family prayers should be revived along with many other good New England customs which some modern radicals may ridicule, but to which they owe all that they possess.

The masses today are getting their real education from the daily newspapers. Many of these newspapers have much good material, but the great effort of the daily press is not to make *producers*, but rather to make *consumers*. The policy of the daily press is not to get people to serve, but rather to get them to buy. Not only is the larger portion of the newspapers given up to advertising, but most of this advertising is of non-essentials, if not of luxuries. With this advertising constantly before the people of the country, it is but natural that the material things should seem of greatest importance. To remedy this situation is a great problem today facing the Christian business men of this country. What shall we do about it?

The first step is to give more thought and attention to people, and to establish more points of contact. Let us do humanly, individually, man to man, what we are trying to do in a great big way. Another method to develop this human resource is to give people responsibility. Moreover, we must do so if the nation is to be truly prosperous.

VII

Boost the Other Fellow

Just as our property is safe only as the other fellow's property is safe, just as our daughter is safe
only as the other fellow's daughter is safe, so it also
is true that in order to develop the human soul in
other men, we have to give those men something.

*

My little girl has a black cat; about once in four
months this cat has kittens. Opposite our place is a
man who has an Airedale dog. When that dog comes
across the street and that cat has no kittens, the cat
immediately "beats it" as fast as she can, with the dog
after her. But when that dog comes across the street
and that cat has the responsibility of some kittens, she
immediately turns on the dog and the *dog* "beats it"
with the cat after him. It is the same dog, the same cat,
and the same backyard; but in one instance the cat has
no responsibilities and in the other case she has. Responsibilities develop faith, vision, courage, initiative,
and other things that make the world go round.

Just as our property is safe, only as the other fellow's property is safe; just as our daughter is safe, only
as the other fellow's daughter is safe; so is it also true
that, in order to develop the human soul in other men,
we have to give those men something. We must give
them a chance. We must give them opportunity. We
must give them a boost. All of us are simply storage
batteries. We get out of life what we put into life. We
care for others, not in accordance with what they do
for us, but rather in accordance with what we have
done for them.

I am quite often asked about investments. Well,
there are times, about once in three or four years —

during panics, when every one is scared to death — that I invest in stocks. There are other times when I advise the purchase of bonds. The fact is, however, that I have not made my money investing either in stocks or bonds. What money I have made has come from investing in boys and girls, young men and young women.

There is a common belief current today that only people with experience are worth while. But I say: Quit looking for the experienced salesmen and trying to make a man out of him; get a *man*, and then make a salesman of him. I have a young man in my business who was delivering trunks for an express company twelve years ago. Today he is my sales manager and has built our gross from $100,000 to $1,000,000. One of my best experts, a man who is sought for by the leading Chambers of Commerce all over the land, was a carpenter on my garage nine years ago. Another one of my experts, a man the demand for whose services I cannot supply, never acquired recognition until he was over forty-five years of age. I found him keeping hens at Wellesley Farms! A young lady in my office to whom I pay $200 a week and who is worth, to me, $1,000 a week, I picked up at $4 a week twelve years ago.

Such cases exist everywhere. You men yourselves know them. You look over your own organizations. Who are the men who are really doing things? Are they the men you acquired ready-made from other concerns? No! They are the men that have been taken up and developed. These are the men that have made money for you and have created the business enterprise of which you are the head. Yet when we have reached a point of prestige, and have a big business, we are tempted to say: "I haven't time to develop any more people, I have got to get them already made." This is a big mistake.

******

I beg my readers — those who have them — to get your foremen together. Say to the partners or the officials of your concern: "Haven't we given too much thought to developing the structure? Aren't we piling too many stories one upon another with too little thought to the foundation?" Then go out and look over your plant and select a few people in each department to whom you will give a real opportunity. Start in to develop them and thereby strengthen the foundation of the business and the prosperity of the nation.

VIII

What Truly Counts

The greatest resources in the world today are human resources, not resources of iron, copper and lumber. The great need of the hour is to strengthen this human foundation and you business men are the one group that can do it.

*

When it comes to the sale of goods, the same principle applies. Eighty per cent. of our sales organizations are devoted to selling to ten per cent. of the population. We have forgotten to consider whether or not goods are needed. We only consider whether or not they are being bought. We are forgetting to establish new markets, but rather are scrambling over the markets already secured. Tremendous opportunities exist in developing new industries, in creating new communities, in relocating the center of production from one community to another community to match up with the center of consumption.

We have forgotten the latent power in the human soul, in the individual, in the community, in the different parts of the country. We have forgotten those human possibilities upon which all prosperity ultimately depends. I cannot perhaps emphasize this any more than by saying that the foundation of progress is spiritual, not material.

The greatest resources of the world today are human resources — not resources of iron, copper and lumber. The great need of the hour is to strengthen this human foundation and revive in men a desire to produce and a joy in service. Business men are the one group that can do it. They understand the emotions, understand the importance of the intangible things. They understand how to awaken in people new motives. So my appeal is not to wait too long to revive man and awaken the soul which is slumbering today.

The nation is only a mass of individuals. The true prosperity of a country depends upon the same qualities as the true prosperity of its people. As religion is necessary for the man, it is also necessary for the nation. As the soul of man needs to be developed, so also does the soul of the nation.

******

Let me tell one more personal incident. Not long ago I was at my Washington office spending the week. While there a little Western Union messenger girl came in to apply for a position. It was in the afternoon — about half-past five. I was struck with the intelligence of the girl's face and asked her two or three questions. She was tired. I asked her to sit down. I was astonished to hear her story.

She had been born and brought up in the mountains of West Virginia — many miles from civilization. Her father and mother died when she was four years old. She had been living with an old grandfather and brother. When I began to talk with her I found her to have a most remarkable acquaintance with Emerson, with Thoreau, with Bernard Shaw and with the old Eastern writers.

I said to her: "How is it that you are delivering telegrams in a khaki suit and a soldier cap?"

She replied: "Because I could get nothing else to do. I lived down there in the mountains just as long as I could. I had to get to the city where I could express myself and develop my finer qualities. When I got to Washington there was nothing that I could do. They asked me if I could typewrite, but I had never seen a typewriter. Finally, after walking the streets for a while, I got a job as a Western Union messenger."

I wrote Mrs. Babson and made arrangements to

have the girl come to Wellesley and work for a few months with the Babson Organization. I saw in her certain qualities which, if developed, should make her very useful to someone somewhere. She came to Wellesley. About a month after her arrival I was obliged to leave on a two months' trip and Mrs. Babson invited her up to dine the night before I left. I told her that I was going to speak while away on "America's Undeveloped Resources." After dinner she went to my desk and took her pen and scribbled these lines and said:

"Perhaps during your talk on America's Greatest Undeveloped Resources you will give those men a message from a Western Union girl." These are the lines she wrote. They are by Ella Wheeler Wilcox.

I gave a beggar from my little store of wealth some gold;
He spent the shining ore, and came again and yet again,
Still cold and hungry, as before.

I gave a thought — and through that thought of mine,
He found himself, the man supreme, divine,
Fed, clothed and crowned with blessing manifold;
And now he begs no more.

The mind of man is a wonderful thing, but unless the soul of man is awakened he must lack faith, power, originality, ambition — those vital elements which make a man a real producer. I do not say that you can awaken this force in every soul. If you are an employer, perhaps only a few of all your employees can be made to understand. But this much is certain — in every man or woman in whom you can loose the power of this invisible something, you will mobilize a force, not only for his or her good, but for the good and perhaps the very salvation of your own business.

IX

What Figures Show

Panics are caused by spiritual causes rather than financial. Prosperity is the result of righteousness rather than of material things.

*

The large black areas on the chart below are formed by combining and plotting current figures on New Building, Crops, Clearings, Immigration, Total Foreign Trade, Money, Failures, Commodity Prices, Railroad Earnings, Stock Prices and Politics in order to give a composite view of business in the United States. (When Interstate Commerce reports of earnings of all United States railroads became available, January, 1909, this record was substituted in place of the earnings of ten representative roads which had been used previous to that time. Revised scales for monetary figures were also introduced, in August, 1912.)

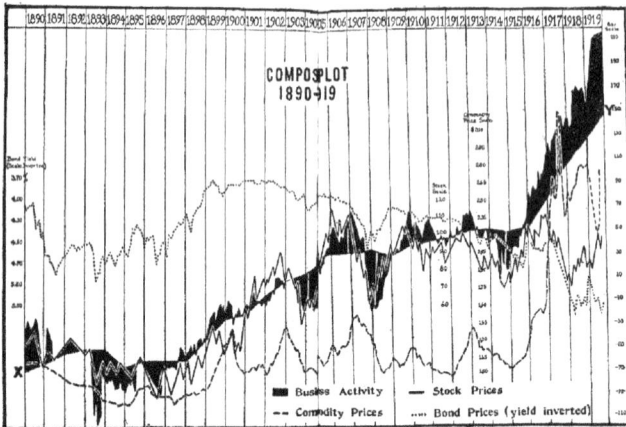

The line X-Y represents the country's net gain or growth. Based on the economic theory that "action and reaction are equal when the two factors of time and intensity are multiplied to form an area," the sums of the areas above and below said line X-Y must, over sufficiently long periods of time, be equal, provided enough subjects are included, properly weighed and combined. An area of prosperity is always followed by an area of depression; an area of depression in turn is always followed by an area of prosperity. The areas, however, need not have the same shapes.

It will be seen that each area is divided into halves by a narrow white line. This is to emphasize the fact that the first halves of areas below the X-Y line are really reactions from the extravagance, inefficiency and corruption which existed during the latter half of the preceding "prosperity" area. Contrariwise, the first halves of areas above the X-Y line are really reactions from the economy, industry and righteousness developed during the hard times just preceding. The high points of the stock market have come in the early part of the prosperity areas and the low points have come about the beginning of the depression areas. In 1914 the war held down prices of all securities. The highest prices of bonds have usually come about the end of the depression areas and high money rates, and lowest bond prices at about the end of the prosperity areas.

But what causes these fluctuations in business and prices? Statistics show that panics are caused by spiritual causes, rather than financial, and that prosperity is the result of righteousness rather than of material things. Hence, the importance to industry and commerce of the forces already mentioned. These spiritual forces are the true fundamentals of prosperity. This in turn leads us to consider from where they come and upon what we are to depend for their further development. The following pages will give the answer.

******

What are the sources of these fundamentals of prosperity? Where do we get this faith, integrity, industry, cooperation and interest in the soul of man upon which civilization is based?

As already explained, we do not get it from the raw materials. We have always had the raw materials. We do not get it from education. From a statistical point of view Germany is the best educated country in the world. It has the least illiteracy. It has the largest percentage of scientific culture. No, these three fundamentals do not come from education. They do not come from the inheritance of property. I mentioned in the preceding pages the investigation we made of leading captains of industry in America, the men who head the various greatest industries in this country. Out of this group of men, only ten per cent. inherited their business, while only fifteen per cent. received special education. This shows that the source of these qualities is from something more than wealth or education.

We are striving and even slaving to lay up property for our children, when statistics clearly show that the more we lay up for them the worse off they are going to be. If statistics demonstrate any one thing, they demonstrate that the less money we leave our children the better off they will be; not only spiritually and physically, but also financially. When it comes to the question of education, we work and economize to give our children an education and to send our children to college. Yet statistics show that only a small percentage of these leading business men are college graduates.

The success of individuals, the success of communities, the success of nations, depends on these fundamentals — integrity, faith, industry, brotherly kindness and an interest in the soul of man. To what do we owe these great fundamental qualities? *Statistics* show clearly that we owe them to religion. Yes, and to the old-fashioned religion of our forefathers. Moreover, I say this not as a churchman. I would give the same message if I were speaking to a group of bankers or a group of engineers. I was first brought into the Church through the Christian Endeavour Society, but I was really converted to the Bible teachings through a study of statistics.

To religion we owe our civilization and to the Church we owe our religion. All there is in the world today that is worth while comes from men filled with, and from groups actuated by, these fundamentals of integrity, faith, industry, brotherly love and those other factors which come only through God. The Church today deserves the credit for keeping these factors before the world. Hence, it is evident that the people of America have not the bankers to thank for their security and prosperity, but rather the preachers and the churches. To these men we are obligated for our growth and development.

X

Where the Church Falls Down

Become saturated with Christ's principles, be clean and upright, cooperate with one another, have faith, serve, trust the Almighty for the results, and you will never have to worry about property. "If you will do these things, all of the others will be given to you."

*

There are two groups of people who criticize the Church. First, there are those who claim great love for their fellow-men, but do not go to church because it is allied with the property interests of the community. I believe that to be the fundamental reason why the wage workers, labour leaders, socialists and radicals are not interested in the Church. They believe that the Church is too closely allied with property. I have been severely criticized myself for presenting the Church as a defender of property and as a means of making your home, your business and your securities safer. Such critics are perfectly conscientious and the Church suffers much because those people, in their love for humanity, are antagonistic to the Church.

The second group are those defenders of property who look upon the Church as impractical; who consider the Golden Rule as something all right for the minister to talk about on Sundays, but something useless to try to follow during the week. Those men criticize the Church for preaching love, for talking the Sermon on the Mount, and for being what they say is "impractical." So the Church suffers today by having both of these groups stand off alone. Neither of them is interested in the Church, the most important organization in America. It is the Church which has created America, which has developed our schools, which has created our homes, which has built our cities, which has developed our industries, which has made our hospitals, charities, and which has done everything that is worth while in America. Yet today, the Church is the most discarded industry of all, because it has not the cooperation of either of the above groups — the radical group which claims to be interested only in humanity and not in property, and the propertied group which frankly says that it is primarily interested in property and not humanity. It seems that we should stop side-stepping this question. Instead we should face it squarely and answer both of these criticisms. My answer is as follows:

Jesus was not interested in property, *per se*. There is no question but that Jesus had no interest in property. These things which look so important to us — houses, roads, taxation, buildings, fields, crops, foreign trade, ships — it is very evident were insignificant to Jesus. When any of Jesus' disciples came to Him to settle some property question, He pushed them aside and said He was too busy to consider it. I am sure that if Jesus were here to-day, He would tell us all that we are idiots for striving so to accumulate things — building ourselves bigger houses, getting bigger bank accounts and more automobiles. Hence, when the socialist or the radical or the labour leader complains to me, I frankly admit this fact. Without doubt the Church should emphasize that property *of itself* is of no value, and the only things worth while in life are happiness and the health and the freedom which come from living an upright, simple life.

On the other hand, and this point I wish to emphasize just as strongly, Jesus took the position throughout His teachings, that if His disciples would simply get saturated with His fundamentals, if they would be clean and upright, if they would cooperate with one another, if they would have faith to serve and trust the Almighty for the results, they would never have to worry about property. Property would take care of itself. Jesus emphasized, first, that they should not think of property; but He always closed His discourses by some such statement as this: "If you will do these things, all of the others will be given to you."

It is absolutely impossible for any individual to develop the above fundamentals of prosperity — faith, integrity, industry and brotherly kindness — without being successful. I care not whether he is a doctor, teacher, banker, lawyer, business man or manufacturer. That same thing is true of groups and of nations. It is fundamental law, "Whatsoever a man soweth that shall he also reap." Those who serve will be served; those who knock will be knocked; those who boost will be boosted. We are paid in the coin that we give. We are forgiven as we forgive. If we are friendly, we will make friends.

Statistics show that the Church is the greatest factor in the worldly success of men, groups and nations. Some readers may have seen a book written by Professor Carver of Harvard entitled, "The Religion Worth Having." In that book the author discusses the various denominations of Christianity. Then he says most conclusively that the religion worth having, the religion that will survive, is the religion which produces the most. Yet this production will not come by seeking production *per se*, but rather by the development of these fundamental characteristics which have been described.

Try as you will you cannot separate the factor of religion from economic development. In the work conducted by my Organization at Wellesley Hills we study the trend of religious interest as closely as we do the condition of the banks or the supply of and demand for commodities. Statistics of church membership form one of the best barometers of business conditions. We have these figures charted back for the past fifty years. Whenever this line of religious interest turns downward and reaches a low level, history shows that it is time to prepare for a reaction and depression in business conditions. Every great panic we have ever had has been foreshadowed by a general decline in observance of religious principles. On the other hand, when the line of religious interest begins to climb and the nation turns again to the simple mode of living laid by in the Bible, then it is time to make ready for a period of business prosperity.

XI

The Future Church

The time is coming when the Church will awake
to its great opportunities. The greatest industry in
America but the most backward and inefficiently
operated, is still in the stage-coach class.

Of course the Church is very far from developed.
The Church is in the same position today as were the
water-powers fifty years ago. The Church has great
resources; but these resources are sadly undeveloped.
From an efficiency point of view, from an organization point of view, from a production point of view,
the Church today is in the stage-coach class. It holds
within itself the keys of prosperity. It holds within
itself the salvation and solution of our industrial,
commercial and international problems. Yet it is
working, or at least the Protestant branch is open,
only three or four hours a week. The Church has the
greatest opportunity today of any industry. It is the
least developed industry, the most inefficiently operated, and the most backward in its methods.

Let us shut our eyes and look ahead at what it will
be twenty-five years from now. Let us imagine five
churches within a radius of five miles. All of them now
operating independently. Each one open only a few
hours a week. Twenty-five years from now these five
churches will be linked up together under a general
manager who will not be a parson, but who will be a
business man.

Today the preacher of our churches is a combination of preacher, business manager, and salesman. He
is the service department, the finance department and
everything but the janitor. The Church is being oper-

ated today as a college would be operated with one professor, who would be president, treasurer, general manager, and everything else. The Church is being operated today as a factory with simply a production man and no one to tend the finances or the sales. Manufacturers reading this book know how long a factory could be run with only a superintendent and no one to sell or finance the proposition.

Twenty-five years from today, instead of the pastor being at the head of the church and a few good people doing voluntary work, there will be four or five churches of the same denomination united under one general manager. I do not mean by this that four of them will be closed. They will all be open much more than they are now; but they will all be under one general manager and will be taking orders from that general manager. Twenty-five years from today the churches will be self-supporting. The days of begging will be over. Religion has been cheapened by singing about "salvation's free for you and me." When we have our legal difficulties, we go to a lawyer and pay him; when we have a pain we go to a doctor and pay him; if we want our children taught we pay the price; but if we want our children instructed in the fundamentals of prosperity upon which their future depends, we send them to a Sunday School for a half-hour a week with the possibility of having them taught by a silly girl who doesn't know her work. In any event the parent seldom takes the trouble to ascertain the quality of the teaching.

The time is coming when the Church will awake to its great principles and opportunities. The greatest industry in America is still the most backward and most inefficiently operated. When these four or five churches are combined, the preacher will not have to spend half the week in preparing a different sermon every Sunday. He will have two weeks or a month to prepare that sermon. He will have time and have the "pep" and energy to deliver it to you so you won't go to sleep while sitting in the pews. The audience will then hear the same preacher only once each month, and the preacher will then have more than one congregation to appeal to.

The same man is not going to be expected to preach on Love, Hate, the League of Nations, How to Settle Labour Disputes and the Health of the Community and every other subject. All of these men will preach the salvation of Jesus, but each one will specialize in one particular phase of the Christian life, such as Faith, Integrity, Industry, Cooperation. Then we will take more stock in our preachers because they won't pretend to know every subject. Then the preacher will not be of lesser intelligence than the average audience.

Fifty years ago the ablest men in every community were the preachers, the doctors, and the lawyers. They were the only college graduates of the town and were looked up to. Today, while we pay our sales managers from $15,000 to $20,000 a year, and lawyers and doctors large fees, we pay our preachers only miserable salaries. It's a damnable disgrace to all of us. I often think that if Jesus were to come back to us, that He would take for His text that thought from the Sermon on the Mount, "If you have aught against your neighbour, before you enter into your worship go and square up." I think that when He came in to speak to us on Sunday morning, He would say:

"Gentlemen, I suggest that before we have this service, we raise funds to pay the preacher a decent salary."

******

Just before I went to Brazil I was the guest of the President of the Argentine Republic. After lunching one day we sat in his sun parlour looking out over the river. He was very thoughtful. He said, "Mr. Babson, I have been wondering why it is that South America with all its great natural advantages is so far behind North America notwithstanding that South America was settled before North America." Then he went on to tell how the forests of South America had two hundred and eighty-six trees that can be found in no book of botany. He told me about many ranches that had thousands of acres under alfalfa in one block. He mentioned the mines of iron, coal, copper, silver, gold; all those great rivers and water-powers which rival Niagara. "Why is it, with all these natural resources, South America is so far behind North America?" he asked. Well, those of you who have been there know the reason. But, being a guest, I said:

"Mr. President, what do you think is the reason?"

He replied: "I have come to this conclusion. South America was settled by the Spanish who came to South America in search of *gold*, but North America was settled by the Pilgrim Fathers who went there in search of *God*."

Friends, let us as American citizens never kick down the ladder by which we climbed up. Let us never forget the foundation upon which all permanent prosperity is based.

THE END

www.ingramcontent.com/pod-product-compliance
Lightning Source LLC
Chambersburg PA
CBHW031617040426
42452CB00006B/564